Goal Write Achieve

BOLD

Goal Write Achieve
BOLD

This journal belongs to

_____

Why do you believe it is important to involve God in your goal-setting process? How does seeking His guidance help you avoid distractions and stay focused on what truly matters?

_____

_____

_____

_____

_____

_____

_____

_____

_____

_____

_____

_____

_____

_____

_____

_____

_____

_____

How does planning with God change the way you view your future? Write about a goal or dream you have and explore how inviting God into the process could lead to greater peace, wisdom, and success.

_____

_____

_____

_____

_____

_____

_____

_____

_____

_____

_____

_____

_____

_____

_____

_____

_____

_____

_____

How could setting goals with God give you confidence in His strength and provision?

_____

_____

_____

_____

_____

_____

_____

_____

_____

_____

_____

_____

_____

_____

_____

_____

_____

_____

_____

BOLD

There is nothing wrong with having goals or working hard to reach those goals.

Goals are important.

Goals help give us a sense of direction, motivate us, and help us stay focused and on track with our purpose. They also aid in building short-term and long-term action plans.

The problem with setting goals is that we often leave God out. One day, God revealed to me that goals should be God On All Levels.

This is powerful.

Here are five reasons why it is important to set goals with God:
1. To align with God's will
2. He provides guidance and clarity
3. It builds our trust in God
4. It increases our humbleness
5. Our goals will have a lasting impact

With God, our goals are achievable beyond what we could ever imagine. So, how do we ensure our goals are GOALs (God On All Levels)? By being BOLD. God gave me this method of goal setting.

BOLD = Big, Obedient, Lasting, Doubtless

Big
Ephesians 3:12 Because of Christ and our faith in him, we can now come boldly and confidently into God's presence.

Ephesians 3:20 Now all glory to God, who is able, through his mighty power at work within us, to accomplish infinitely more than we might ask or think.

We can approach God with bold assurance because God will do more than we could think.

Obedient

Luke 11:28 Jesus replied, "But even more blessed are all who hear the word of God and put it into practice."

Your goals must align with what God is saying and has called you to do.

Lasting

Matthew 5:13

You are the salt of the earth. But what good is salt if it has lost its flavor? Can you make it salty again? It will be thrown out and trampled underfoot as worthless.

As salt loses its flavor and becomes useless, your goals will do the same when they are not aligned with God. Losing sight of your purpose can lead to a lack of fulfillment. You should regularly assess your goals to ensure they reflect your God-given purpose.

Doubtless

James 1:6

But when you ask him, be sure that your faith is in God alone. Do not waver, for a person with divided loyalty is as unsettled as a wave of the sea that is blown and tossed by the wind.

You must not be divided or double-minded in goal setting. You must stay committed, steadfast, and trust what God has purposed you to do.

You should develop objectives to help you stay on track with your goals. Objectives are developed from goals. Objectives are the specific steps you will take to reach your goals.

Use this journal to plan your goals with God.

What's Inside?
Goal pages
Objectives
Goal Prayer
Priority Matrix
Goal Resources
Goal Reflection

Setting and Pursuing Goals

Below are a few scriptures about goals.

1. Proverbs 16:3 - "Commit your works to the Lord [submit and trust them to Him], And your plans will succeed [if you respond to His will and guidance]."
2. Philippians 3:14 - "I press on toward the goal to win the [heavenly] prize of the upward call of God in Christ Jesus."
3. Proverbs 21:5 - "The plans of the diligent lead surely to abundance and advantage, But everyone who acts in haste comes surely to poverty."
4. Proverbs 4:25-27 - "Let your eyes look directly ahead [toward the path of moral courage] And let your gaze be fixed straight in front of you [toward the path of integrity]. Consider well and watch carefully the path of your feet, And all your ways will be steadfast and sure. Do not turn away to the right nor to the left [where evil may lurk]; Turn your foot from [the path of] evil."
5. Habakkuk 2:2-3 - "Then the Lord answered me and said, "Write the vision And engrave it plainly on [clay] tablets So that the one who reads it will run. For the vision is yet for the appointed [future] time It hurries toward the goal [of fulfillment]; it will not fail. Even though it delays, wait [patiently] for it, Because it will certainly come; it will not delay."

The Holy Bible: The Amplified Bible. 1987. 2015. La Habra, CA: The Lockman Foundation.

Goal

_____

_____

What makes your goal Big?

What makes your goal obedient?

What makes your goal lasting?

What makes your goal Doubtless?

Objectives

Write down the steps you need to take to reach your goal.

1. _____

2. _____

3. _____

4. _____

5. _____

6. _____

7. _____

8. _____

9. _____

10. _____

11. _____

12. _____

13. _____

14. _____

15. _____

Priority Matrix
use this matrix to prioritize your objectives.

<u>Most Important Has Deadlines</u>

<u>Important Has No Deadlines</u>

<u>Want To Do</u>

<u>Not Necessary To Do</u>

Goal Resources

Important Scriptures

- [ ] _____
- [ ] _____
- [ ] _____
- [ ] _____
- [ ] _____
- [ ] _____
- [ ] _____
- [ ] _____
- [ ] _____
- [ ] _____
- [ ] _____
- [ ] _____

Websites, Training & Education

- [ ] _____
- [ ] _____
- [ ] _____
- [ ] _____
- [ ] _____
- [ ] _____
- [ ] _____
- [ ] _____
- [ ] _____
- [ ] _____
- [ ] _____

Contacts

- [ ] _____
- [ ] _____
- [ ] _____
- [ ] _____
- [ ] _____
- [ ] _____
- [ ] _____
- [ ] _____
- [ ] _____
- [ ] _____
- [ ] _____
- [ ] _____
- [ ] _____

Financial

- [ ] _____
- [ ] _____
- [ ] _____
- [ ] _____
- [ ] _____
- [ ] _____
- [ ] _____
- [ ] _____
- [ ] _____
- [ ] _____
- [ ] _____

Goal Notes

_____

_____

_____

_____

_____

_____

_____

_____

_____

_____

_____

_____

_____

_____

_____

_____

_____

_____

Goal Reflection

Use this page to reflect on planning your goal with God, goal achievement, and anything else you experienced during this goal period.

_____

_____

_____

_____

_____

_____

_____

_____

_____

_____

_____

_____

_____

_____

_____

_____

_____

_____

_____

Goal

_____

_____

What makes your goal Big?

What makes your goal obedient?

What makes your goal lasting?

What makes your goal Doubtless?

Objectives

Write down the steps you need to take to reach your goal.

1. _____

2. _____

3. _____

4. _____

5. _____

6. _____

7. _____

8. _____

9. _____

10. _____

11. _____

12. _____

13. _____

14. _____

15. _____

Priority Matrix

use this matrix to prioritize your objectives.

Most Important Has Deadlines

Important Has No Deadlines

Want To Do

Not Necessary To Do

Goal Resources

Important Scriptures

- [ ] _____
- [ ] _____
- [ ] _____
- [ ] _____
- [ ] _____
- [ ] _____
- [ ] _____
- [ ] _____
- [ ] _____
- [ ] _____
- [ ] _____
- [ ] _____
- [ ] _____

Websites, Training & Education

- [ ] _____
- [ ] _____
- [ ] _____
- [ ] _____
- [ ] _____
- [ ] _____
- [ ] _____
- [ ] _____
- [ ] _____
- [ ] _____
- [ ] _____
- [ ] _____
- [ ] _____

Contacts

- [ ] _____
- [ ] _____
- [ ] _____
- [ ] _____
- [ ] _____
- [ ] _____
- [ ] _____
- [ ] _____
- [ ] _____
- [ ] _____
- [ ] _____
- [ ] _____
- [ ] _____

Financial

- [ ] _____
- [ ] _____
- [ ] _____
- [ ] _____
- [ ] _____
- [ ] _____
- [ ] _____
- [ ] _____
- [ ] _____
- [ ] _____
- [ ] _____
- [ ] _____

Goal Notes

Goal Reflection

Use this page to reflect on planning your goal with God, goal achievement, and anything else you experienced during this goal period.

_____

_____

_____

_____

_____

_____

_____

_____

_____

_____

_____

_____

_____

_____

_____

_____

_____

_____

Goal

_____

_____

What makes your goal Big?

What makes your goal obedient?

What makes your goal lasting?

What makes your goal Doubtless?

Objectives

Write down the steps you need to take to reach your goal.

1. _____

2. _____

3. _____

4. _____

5. _____

6. _____

7. _____

8. _____

9. _____

10. _____

11. _____

12. _____

13. _____

14. _____

15. _____

Priority Matrix
use this matrix to prioritize your objectives.

<u>Most Important Has Deadlines</u>

<u>Important Has No Deadlines</u>

<u>Want To Do</u>

<u>Not Necessary To Do</u>

Goal Resources

Important Scriptures

- [ ] _____
- [ ] _____
- [ ] _____
- [ ] _____
- [ ] _____
- [ ] _____
- [ ] _____
- [ ] _____
- [ ] _____
- [ ] _____
- [ ] _____
- [ ] _____

Websites, Training & Education

- [ ] _____
- [ ] _____
- [ ] _____
- [ ] _____
- [ ] _____
- [ ] _____
- [ ] _____
- [ ] _____
- [ ] _____
- [ ] _____
- [ ] _____
- [ ] _____

Contacts

- [ ] _____
- [ ] _____
- [ ] _____
- [ ] _____
- [ ] _____
- [ ] _____
- [ ] _____
- [ ] _____
- [ ] _____
- [ ] _____
- [ ] _____
- [ ] _____

Financial

- [ ] _____
- [ ] _____
- [ ] _____
- [ ] _____
- [ ] _____
- [ ] _____
- [ ] _____
- [ ] _____
- [ ] _____
- [ ] _____
- [ ] _____

Goal Notes

_____

_____

_____

_____

_____

_____

_____

_____

_____

_____

_____

_____

_____

_____

_____

_____

_____

_____

_____

Goal Reflection

Use this page to reflect on planning your goal with God, goal achievement, and anything else you experienced during this goal period.

_____

_____

_____

_____

_____

_____

_____

_____

_____

_____

_____

_____

_____

_____

_____

_____

_____

_____

_____

_____

Goal

_____

_____

What makes your goal Big?

What makes your goal obedient?

What makes your goal lasting?

What makes your goal Doubtless?

Objectives

Write down the steps you need to take to reach your goal.

1. _____

2. _____

3. _____

4. _____

5. _____

6. _____

7. _____

8. _____

9. _____

10. _____

11. _____

12. _____

13. _____

14. _____

15. _____

Priority Matrix

use this matrix to prioritize your objectives.

<u>Most Important Has Deadlines</u>

<u>Important Has No Deadlines</u>

<u>Want To Do</u>

<u>Not Necessary To Do</u>

Goal Resources

Important Scriptures

- [ ] _____
- [ ] _____
- [ ] _____
- [ ] _____
- [ ] _____
- [ ] _____
- [ ] _____
- [ ] _____
- [ ] _____
- [ ] _____
- [ ] _____
- [ ] _____

Websites, Training & Education

- [ ] _____
- [ ] _____
- [ ] _____
- [ ] _____
- [ ] _____
- [ ] _____
- [ ] _____
- [ ] _____
- [ ] _____
- [ ] _____
- [ ] _____

Contacts

- [ ] _____
- [ ] _____
- [ ] _____
- [ ] _____
- [ ] _____
- [ ] _____
- [ ] _____
- [ ] _____
- [ ] _____
- [ ] _____
- [ ] _____
- [ ] _____

Financial

- [ ] _____
- [ ] _____
- [ ] _____
- [ ] _____
- [ ] _____
- [ ] _____
- [ ] _____
- [ ] _____
- [ ] _____
- [ ] _____

Goal Notes

_____

_____

_____

_____

_____

_____

_____

_____

_____

_____

_____

_____

_____

_____

_____

_____

_____

_____

_____

_____

Goal Reflection

Use this page to reflect on planning your goal with God, goal achievement, and anything else you experienced during this goal period.

_____

_____

_____

_____

_____

_____

_____

_____

_____

_____

_____

_____

_____

_____

_____

_____

_____

_____

_____

Goal

_____

_____

what makes your goal Big?

what makes your goal obedient?

what makes your goal lasting?

What makes your goal Doubtless?

Objectives

Write down the steps you need to take to reach your goal.

1. _____

2. _____

3. _____

4. _____

5. _____

6. _____

7. _____

8. _____

9. _____

10. _____

11. _____

12. _____

13. _____

14. _____

15. _____

Priority Matrix
use this matrix to prioritize your objectives.

Most Important Has Deadlines	Important Has No Deadlines
Want To Do	Not Necessary To Do

Goal Resources

Important Scriptures

- ☐ _____
- ☐ _____
- ☐ _____
- ☐ _____
- ☐ _____
- ☐ _____
- ☐ _____
- ☐ _____
- ☐ _____
- ☐ _____
- ☐ _____
- ☐ _____

Websites, Training & Education

- ☐ _____
- ☐ _____
- ☐ _____
- ☐ _____
- ☐ _____
- ☐ _____
- ☐ _____
- ☐ _____
- ☐ _____
- ☐ _____
- ☐ _____
- ☐ _____

Contacts

- ☐ _____
- ☐ _____
- ☐ _____
- ☐ _____
- ☐ _____
- ☐ _____
- ☐ _____
- ☐ _____
- ☐ _____
- ☐ _____
- ☐ _____
- ☐ _____
- ☐ _____

Financial

- ☐ _____
- ☐ _____
- ☐ _____
- ☐ _____
- ☐ _____
- ☐ _____
- ☐ _____
- ☐ _____
- ☐ _____
- ☐ _____
- ☐ _____
- ☐ _____
- ☐ _____

Goal Notes

_____

_____

_____

_____

_____

_____

_____

_____

_____

_____

_____

_____

_____

_____

_____

_____

_____

_____

Goal Reflection

Use this page to reflect on planning your goal with God, goal achievement, and anything else you experienced during this goal period.

_____

_____

_____

_____

_____

_____

_____

_____

_____

_____

_____

_____

_____

_____

_____

_____

_____

_____

Goal

_____

_____

What makes your goal Big?

What makes your goal obedient?

What makes your goal lasting?

What makes your goal Doubtless?

Objectives

Write down the steps you need to take to reach your goal.

1. _____

2. _____

3. _____

4. _____

5. _____

6. _____

7. _____

8. _____

9. _____

10. _____

11. _____

12. _____

13. _____

14. _____

15. _____

Priority Matrix

use this matrix to prioritize your objectives.

Most Important Has Deadlines

Important Has No Deadlines

Want To Do

Not Necessary To Do

Goal Resources

Important Scriptures

- [ ] _____
- [ ] _____
- [ ] _____
- [ ] _____
- [ ] _____
- [ ] _____
- [ ] _____
- [ ] _____
- [ ] _____
- [ ] _____
- [ ] _____
- [ ] _____
- [ ] _____

Websites, Training & Education

- [ ] _____
- [ ] _____
- [ ] _____
- [ ] _____
- [ ] _____
- [ ] _____
- [ ] _____
- [ ] _____
- [ ] _____
- [ ] _____
- [ ] _____
- [ ] _____
- [ ] _____

Contacts

- [ ] _____
- [ ] _____
- [ ] _____
- [ ] _____
- [ ] _____
- [ ] _____
- [ ] _____
- [ ] _____
- [ ] _____
- [ ] _____
- [ ] _____
- [ ] _____
- [ ] _____

Financial

- [ ] _____
- [ ] _____
- [ ] _____
- [ ] _____
- [ ] _____
- [ ] _____
- [ ] _____
- [ ] _____
- [ ] _____
- [ ] _____
- [ ] _____

Goal Notes

Goal Reflection

Use this page to reflect on planning your goal with God, goal achievement, and anything else you experienced during this goal period.

_____

_____

_____

_____

_____

_____

_____

_____

_____

_____

_____

_____

_____

_____

_____

_____

_____

_____

Goal

_____

_____

What makes your goal Big?

What makes your goal obedient?

What makes your goal lasting?

What makes your goal Doubtless?

Objectives

Write down the steps you need to take to reach your goal.

1._____

2._____

3._____

4._____

5._____

6._____

7._____

8._____

9._____

10._____

11._____

12._____

13._____

14._____

15._____

Priority Matrix

use this matrix to prioritize your objectives.

<u>Most Important Has Deadlines</u>

<u>Important Has No Deadlines</u>

<u>Want To Do</u>

<u>Not Necessary To Do</u>

Goal Resources

Important Scriptures

- ☐ _____
- ☐ _____
- ☐ _____
- ☐ _____
- ☐ _____
- ☐ _____
- ☐ _____
- ☐ _____
- ☐ _____
- ☐ _____
- ☐ _____
- ☐ _____

Websites, Training & Education

- ☐ _____
- ☐ _____
- ☐ _____
- ☐ _____
- ☐ _____
- ☐ _____
- ☐ _____
- ☐ _____
- ☐ _____
- ☐ _____
- ☐ _____
- ☐ _____

Contacts

- ☐ _____
- ☐ _____
- ☐ _____
- ☐ _____
- ☐ _____
- ☐ _____
- ☐ _____
- ☐ _____
- ☐ _____
- ☐ _____
- ☐ _____
- ☐ _____

Financial

- ☐ _____
- ☐ _____
- ☐ _____
- ☐ _____
- ☐ _____
- ☐ _____
- ☐ _____
- ☐ _____
- ☐ _____
- ☐ _____
- ☐ _____

Goal Notes

_____

_____

_____

_____

_____

_____

_____

_____

_____

_____

_____

_____

_____

_____

_____

_____

_____

_____

_____

Goal Reflection

Use this page to reflect on planning your goal with God, goal achievement, and anything else you experienced during this goal period.

_____

_____

_____

_____

_____

_____

_____

_____

_____

_____

_____

_____

_____

_____

_____

_____

_____

_____

_____

Goal

_____

_____

What makes your goal Big?

What makes your goal obedient?

What makes your goal lasting?

What makes your goal Doubtless?

Objectives

Write down the steps you need to take to reach your goal.

1. _____

2. _____

3. _____

4. _____

5. _____

6. _____

7. _____

8. _____

9. _____

10. _____

11. _____

12. _____

13. _____

14. _____

15. _____

Priority Matrix

use this matrix to prioritize your objectives.

Most Important Has Deadlines

Important Has No Deadlines

Want To Do

Not Necessary To Do

Goal Resources

Important Scriptures

- [ ] _____
- [ ] _____
- [ ] _____
- [ ] _____
- [ ] _____
- [ ] _____
- [ ] _____
- [ ] _____
- [ ] _____
- [ ] _____
- [ ] _____
- [ ] _____
- [ ] _____

Websites, Training & Education

- [ ] _____
- [ ] _____
- [ ] _____
- [ ] _____
- [ ] _____
- [ ] _____
- [ ] _____
- [ ] _____
- [ ] _____
- [ ] _____
- [ ] _____
- [ ] _____
- [ ] _____

Contacts

- [ ] _____
- [ ] _____
- [ ] _____
- [ ] _____
- [ ] _____
- [ ] _____
- [ ] _____
- [ ] _____
- [ ] _____
- [ ] _____
- [ ] _____
- [ ] _____
- [ ] _____

Financial

- [ ] _____
- [ ] _____
- [ ] _____
- [ ] _____
- [ ] _____
- [ ] _____
- [ ] _____
- [ ] _____
- [ ] _____
- [ ] _____
- [ ] _____
- [ ] _____
- [ ] _____

Goal Notes

_____

_____

_____

_____

_____

_____

_____

_____

_____

_____

_____

_____

_____

_____

_____

_____

_____

_____

_____

Goal Reflection

Use this page to reflect on planning your goal with God, goal achievement, and anything else you experienced during this goal period.

_____

_____

_____

_____

_____

_____

_____

_____

_____

_____

_____

_____

_____

_____

_____

_____

_____

_____

Goal

_____

_____

What makes your goal Big?

What makes your goal obedient?

What makes your goal lasting?

What makes your goal Doubtless?

Objectives

Write down the steps you need to take to reach your goal.

1. _____

2. _____

3. _____

4. _____

5. _____

6. _____

7. _____

8. _____

9. _____

10. _____

11. _____

12. _____

13. _____

14. _____

15. _____

Priority Matrix
use this matrix to prioritize your objectives.

Most Important Has Deadlines	Important Has No Deadlines

Want To Do	Not Necessary To Do

Goal Resources

Important Scriptures

- ☐ _____
- ☐ _____
- ☐ _____
- ☐ _____
- ☐ _____
- ☐ _____
- ☐ _____
- ☐ _____
- ☐ _____
- ☐ _____
- ☐ _____
- ☐ _____

Websites, Training & Education

- ☐ _____
- ☐ _____
- ☐ _____
- ☐ _____
- ☐ _____
- ☐ _____
- ☐ _____
- ☐ _____
- ☐ _____
- ☐ _____
- ☐ _____
- ☐ _____

Contacts

- ☐ _____
- ☐ _____
- ☐ _____
- ☐ _____
- ☐ _____
- ☐ _____
- ☐ _____
- ☐ _____
- ☐ _____
- ☐ _____
- ☐ _____
- ☐ _____

Financial

- ☐ _____
- ☐ _____
- ☐ _____
- ☐ _____
- ☐ _____
- ☐ _____
- ☐ _____
- ☐ _____
- ☐ _____
- ☐ _____
- ☐ _____
- ☐ _____

Goal Notes

_____

_____

_____

_____

_____

_____

_____

_____

_____

_____

_____

_____

_____

_____

_____

_____

_____

_____

_____

Goal Reflection

Use this page to reflect on planning your goal with God, goal achievement, and anything else you experienced during this goal period.

_____

_____

_____

_____

_____

_____

_____

_____

_____

_____

_____

_____

_____

_____

_____

_____

_____

_____

Goal

_____

_____

What makes your goal Big?

What makes your goal obedient?

What makes your goal lasting?

What makes your goal Doubtless?

Objectives

Write down the steps you need to take to reach your goal.

1. _____
2. _____
3. _____
4. _____
5. _____
6. _____
7. _____
8. _____
9. _____
10. _____
11. _____
12. _____
13. _____
14. _____
15. _____

Priority Matrix

use this matrix to prioritize your objectives.

Most Important Has Deadlines

Important Has No Deadlines

Want To Do

Not Necessary To Do

Goal Resources

Important Scriptures

- [ ] _____
- [ ] _____
- [ ] _____
- [ ] _____
- [ ] _____
- [ ] _____
- [ ] _____
- [ ] _____
- [ ] _____
- [ ] _____
- [ ] _____
- [ ] _____
- [ ] _____

Websites, Training & Education

- [ ] _____
- [ ] _____
- [ ] _____
- [ ] _____
- [ ] _____
- [ ] _____
- [ ] _____
- [ ] _____
- [ ] _____
- [ ] _____
- [ ] _____
- [ ] _____
- [ ] _____

Contacts

- [ ] _____
- [ ] _____
- [ ] _____
- [ ] _____
- [ ] _____
- [ ] _____
- [ ] _____
- [ ] _____
- [ ] _____
- [ ] _____
- [ ] _____
- [ ] _____
- [ ] _____

Financial

- [ ] _____
- [ ] _____
- [ ] _____
- [ ] _____
- [ ] _____
- [ ] _____
- [ ] _____
- [ ] _____
- [ ] _____
- [ ] _____
- [ ] _____

Goal Notes

Goal Reflection

Use this page to reflect on planning your goal with God, goal achievement, and anything else you experienced during this goal period.

_____

_____

_____

_____

_____

_____

_____

_____

_____

_____

_____

_____

_____

_____

_____

_____

_____

_____

_____

Goal

_____

_____

What makes your goal Big?

What makes your goal obedient?

What makes your goal lasting?

What makes your goal Doubtless?

Objectives

Write down the steps you need to take to reach your goal.

1. _____

2. _____

3. _____

4. _____

5. _____

6. _____

7. _____

8. _____

9. _____

10. _____

11. _____

12. _____

13. _____

14. _____

15. _____

Priority Matrix
use this matrix to prioritize your objectives.

<u>Most Important Has Deadlines</u>

<u>Important Has No Deadlines</u>

<u>Want To Do</u>

<u>Not Necessary To Do</u>

Goal Resources

Important Scriptures

- [ ] _____
- [ ] _____
- [ ] _____
- [ ] _____
- [ ] _____
- [ ] _____
- [ ] _____
- [ ] _____
- [ ] _____
- [ ] _____
- [ ] _____
- [ ] _____
- [ ] _____

Websites, Training & Education

- [ ] _____
- [ ] _____
- [ ] _____
- [ ] _____
- [ ] _____
- [ ] _____
- [ ] _____
- [ ] _____
- [ ] _____
- [ ] _____
- [ ] _____
- [ ] _____
- [ ] _____

Contacts

- [ ] _____
- [ ] _____
- [ ] _____
- [ ] _____
- [ ] _____
- [ ] _____
- [ ] _____
- [ ] _____
- [ ] _____
- [ ] _____
- [ ] _____
- [ ] _____
- [ ] _____

Financial

- [ ] _____
- [ ] _____
- [ ] _____
- [ ] _____
- [ ] _____
- [ ] _____
- [ ] _____
- [ ] _____
- [ ] _____
- [ ] _____
- [ ] _____
- [ ] _____

Goal Notes

_____

_____

_____

_____

_____

_____

_____

_____

_____

_____

_____

_____

_____

_____

_____

_____

_____

_____

Goal Reflection

Use this page to reflect on planning your goal with God, goal achievement, and anything else you experienced during this goal period.

_____

_____

_____

_____

_____

_____

_____

_____

_____

_____

_____

_____

_____

_____

_____

_____

_____

_____

Goal

_____

_____

What makes your goal Big?

[ ]

What makes your goal obedient?

[ ]

What makes your goal lasting?

[ ]

What makes your goal Doubtless?

Objectives

Write down the steps you need to take to reach your goal.

1. _____
2. _____
3. _____
4. _____
5. _____
6. _____
7. _____
8. _____
9. _____
10. _____
11. _____
12. _____
13. _____
14. _____
15. _____

Priority Matrix
use this matrix to prioritize your objectives.

Most Important Has Deadlines

Important Has No Deadlines

Want To Do

Not Necessary To Do

Goal Resources

Important Scriptures

- ☐ _____
- ☐ _____
- ☐ _____
- ☐ _____
- ☐ _____
- ☐ _____
- ☐ _____
- ☐ _____
- ☐ _____
- ☐ _____
- ☐ _____
- ☐ _____

Websites, Training & Education

- ☐ _____
- ☐ _____
- ☐ _____
- ☐ _____
- ☐ _____
- ☐ _____
- ☐ _____
- ☐ _____
- ☐ _____
- ☐ _____
- ☐ _____
- ☐ _____

Contacts

- ☐ _____
- ☐ _____
- ☐ _____
- ☐ _____
- ☐ _____
- ☐ _____
- ☐ _____
- ☐ _____
- ☐ _____
- ☐ _____
- ☐ _____
- ☐ _____

Financial

- ☐ _____
- ☐ _____
- ☐ _____
- ☐ _____
- ☐ _____
- ☐ _____
- ☐ _____
- ☐ _____
- ☐ _____
- ☐ _____
- ☐ _____

Goal Notes

_____

_____

_____

_____

_____

_____

_____

_____

_____

_____

_____

_____

_____

_____

_____

_____

_____

_____

Goal Reflection

Use this page to reflect on planning your goal with God, goal achievement, and anything else you experienced during this goal period.

_____

_____

_____

_____

_____

_____

_____

_____

_____

_____

_____

_____

_____

_____

_____

_____

_____

Goal

_____

_____

What makes your goal Big?

What makes your goal obedient?

What makes your goal lasting?

What makes your goal Doubtless?

Objectives

Write down the steps you need to take to reach your goal.

1. _____

2. _____

3. _____

4. _____

5. _____

6. _____

7. _____

8. _____

9. _____

10. _____

11. _____

12. _____

13. _____

14. _____

15. _____

Priority Matrix
use this matrix to prioritize your objectives.

<u>Most Important Has Deadlines</u>

<u>Important Has No Deadlines</u>

<u>Want To Do</u>

<u>Not Necessary To Do</u>

Goal Resources

Important Scriptures

- [ ] _____
- [ ] _____
- [ ] _____
- [ ] _____
- [ ] _____
- [ ] _____
- [ ] _____
- [ ] _____
- [ ] _____
- [ ] _____
- [ ] _____
- [ ] _____
- [ ] _____

Websites, Training & Education

- [ ] _____
- [ ] _____
- [ ] _____
- [ ] _____
- [ ] _____
- [ ] _____
- [ ] _____
- [ ] _____
- [ ] _____
- [ ] _____
- [ ] _____
- [ ] _____

Contacts

- [ ] _____
- [ ] _____
- [ ] _____
- [ ] _____
- [ ] _____
- [ ] _____
- [ ] _____
- [ ] _____
- [ ] _____
- [ ] _____
- [ ] _____
- [ ] _____

Financial

- [ ] _____
- [ ] _____
- [ ] _____
- [ ] _____
- [ ] _____
- [ ] _____
- [ ] _____
- [ ] _____
- [ ] _____
- [ ] _____
- [ ] _____

Goal Notes

_____

_____

_____

_____

_____

_____

_____

_____

_____

_____

_____

_____

_____

_____

_____

_____

_____

Goal Reflection

Use this page to reflect on planning your goal with God, goal achievement, and anything else you experienced during this goal period.

_____

_____

_____

_____

_____

_____

_____

_____

_____

_____

_____

_____

_____

_____

_____

_____

_____

_____

_____